The SILVERSMITHS

*A pine tree shilling, so named for the picture
stamped on the obverse side, one of many made by
the Massachusetts mint in the seventeenth century.*

COLONIAL CRAFTSMEN

The
SILVERSMITHS

WRITTEN & ILLUSTRATED BY

Leonard Everett Fisher

BENCHMARK BOOKS

MARSHALL CAVENDISH
NEW YORK

Benchmark Books
Marshall Cavendish Corporation
99 White Plains Road
Tarrytown, New York 10591-9001

Copyright © 1964 by Leonard Everett Fisher

First Marshall Cavendish edition 1997

Library of Congress Cataloging-in-Publication Data
Fisher, Leonard Everett.
The silversmiths / written & illustrated by Leonard Everett Fisher.
p.   cm. — (Colonial craftsmen)
Originally published: New York : F. Watts, 1964
Includes index.
Summary: Examines the art of the silversmith in colonial times.
ISBN 0-7614-0478-3 (library binding)
1. Silverwork—United States—Juvenile literature. 2. Silverwork, Colonial—United
States—Juvenile literature. [1. Silverwork. 2. United States—History—Colonial period,
ca. 1600–1775.] I. Title. II. Series: Fisher, Leonard Everett. Colonial craftsmen.
NK7112.F57   1997   739.2'3773—dc20   96-16607   CIP   AC

Printed and bound in the United States of America

5   6   4

Other titles in this series

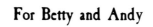

For Betty and Andy

A Short History

An Englishman in the New World.

I N 1630, Puritans from England founded the village of Boston on the shores of New England. This colony was one of the few tiny specks of civilization in the enormous wilderness called America. But within twenty years, Boston had become an important place in the New World. Whole families, seeking a new life in America, arrived in Boston with every ship. Nearly every Englishman traveling to America in the year 1652 headed for Boston.

The rapid growth of the town led to the increase of business, the buying and selling of goods. People did some of their business by bartering, or trading, one type of goods for another, but they also had to have money to carry on their commercial affairs. They had brought some silver money with them to the new land, but not enough to be of much use.

England issued plenty of paper money for her colonists, but it had uncertain value. Silver, on the other hand, had definite value. Silver coins had value. People thought of silver as treasure, and treasure was worth something. But not paper money! Paper was paper, and that was all it was.

Heading for Boston.

The people wanted silver money, not paper money.

England was not anxious to have many silver coins circulating in her colonies. If the colonists had more silver than paper to spend and save, they would surely become richer and more difficult to manage.

But if the colonists did *not* have more silver to spend and save, they would become unruly. England had no choice but to send the colonists more silver money — enough to satisfy them, but not enough to make them rich.

As time went on, a variety of silver coins began to appear. There were English coins of the realm. There were foreign coins of every description, brought in by sea captains and sailors. There were counterfeit coins, made by dishonest people.

Many of the foreign coins did not contain as much silver as English coins did. Many people did not trust them.

No one cared for counterfeit coins. They were absolutely worthless.

A louis: France, 1643.

A dollar: the Netherlands, 1601.

A taler: Denmark, 1624.

A crown: Great Britain, 1604.

13

Most of all, everyone wanted English silver money. And there was not enough of it to meet the growing demand.

The colonists asked England for more silver money. The Government said no. England was in turmoil. Oliver Cromwell and Charles II were fighting each other for power. The colonists asked for permission to make, or mint, their own official coins. The last thing anyone in England wanted was a mint in Massachusetts. Besides, it was against the law for colonies to mint their own coins. Nevertheless, no one paid any attention to the people of Boston. They were unable to get an answer to their request, one way or the other.

The colonists could not wait for an answer. They set up their own mint in Boston, in defiance of English law. It was one of the first acts of defiance by English colonists on their long road to independence. The time was 1652, one hundred and twenty-four years before the Declaration of Independence.

John Hull was appointed manager, or *master*, of the mint. In return for his services, Hull re-

ceived one silver shilling for every twenty he coined. He became a rich and important man.

John Hull was not merely the mintmaster. He was a silversmith, as well — probably the very first silversmith to learn his craft in the American colonies. He was trained in the shop of his older half brother, Richard Storer. Storer himself had learned his work in England under the strict rules of a society of craftsmen, or *guild,* called The Worshipful Company of Goldsmiths of the City of London. This guild had been started four hundred years before any Englishmen settled in America. It was founded in order to keep up the highest quality of craftsmanship in working silver, as well as gold.

The mint in Massachusetts produced good-quality silver coins for thirty-two years before it was closed. Colonial business grew, and the people prospered. But they did not have any savings banks. They needed a way to keep their money safe. Again they turned to the silversmiths for help.

These craftsmen melted down the silver coins and removed their impurities. Then they fash-

*Catching a thief with
the goods — a candlestick struck
with a mark that proves
its ownership.*

ioned the metal into bowls or other useful objects, which still had the original value of the metal from which they were made. Each one was worth its weight in silver. It was not only as good as money — it *was* money. A piece of land could be purchased with a silver bowl, provided that the amount of silver in the bowl was equal in value to the asking price of the land.

Moreover, everyone thought, it might be more difficult for a thief to make off with a silver candlestick than with a pouch of coins. An owner could not prove that coins belonged to him, but he might be able to prove that a candlestick did. The silversmith always "struck his mark" on the piece. That is to say, he always hammered his initials or name on it. The mark of the silversmith not only identified him — and possibly the owner of the piece — but it was also a guarantee of high quality.

The colonial silversmith was not only a skilled craftsman, but he was also a banker, or the nearest thing to it.

All over the colonies, people turned their savings into silver bowls, spoons, cups, mugs, por-

ringers, inkstands, candlesticks, tankards, and later, coffeepots, teapots, and strainers. All this silver was handed down from mothers and fathers to daughters and sons.

The HISTORY

Not all colonial silversmiths were descended from Englishmen. Some, like Cornelius Vanderburgh and Myer Myers, of New York, were Dutch. Some, like Apollos De Rivoire, the father of Paul Revere of Boston, were French. Paul Revere himself, while widely known for his famous ride on the eve of the American Revolution, is also famous as an expert silversmith.

No matter where they came from, the colonial silversmiths were well-trained, careful craftsmen. Their wonderful skill assured the American public of honest practice and high quality.

A teapot, made by Paul Revere, Boston.

A porringer,
made by John de Nise,
Philadelphia.

A candlestick,
made by Jacob Hurd, Boston.

A bowl,
made by Cornelius Kierstede,
New York and New Haven.

21

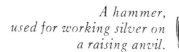
A hammer,
used for working silver on
a raising anvil.

How the
Silversmiths Worked

A SILVERSMITH'S TOOLS

A graver,
used for engraving
decorative designs
on a silver piece.

Shears, used
in cutting silver plate.

A ladle,
used in handling melted silver.

Tongs,
used for holding silver
during reheating.

SILVER IS A SOFT METAL USUally found beneath the ground. To be of any use, it must be dug, or mined. But in colonial times the great North American silver deposits lay undiscovered in the earth. The colonial silversmiths had to rely chiefly on coins — or sometimes on unfashionable or unwanted silver objects — as their source of pure silver.

Silver coins, however, were not made wholly of silver. They contained varying amounts of other metals to make them hard and durable. Some coins contained large amounts of silver. Other coins had very little. It did not matter to the silversmith which coin contained the most silver. His interest was that after all the other metals or impurities were removed, enough pure silver remained to make a bowl or some other useful object.

It did matter to the customer how much pure metal was in the coins he handed to the silversmith. Unless the customer knew this, he could not be sure how much silver was "invested" in the object.

The *TECHNIQUE*

A colonial silversmith's shop.

The *TECHNIQUE*

The first order of business, then, was for the silversmith to weigh the coins so that the amount of silver might be determined. This he did in the presence of the customer. Next, the two talked about the kind of piece that could be made from the amount of silver on hand. After reaching an agreement, the customer left the shop, and the silversmith turned to his furnace to prepare for the exacting tasks ahead.

The coins were placed in shallow cups called *boiling pans,* which were then placed on the hearth of a specially built *refining furnace.* The terrific heat of the furnace melted the coins, and the silversmith could then separate the pure metal from most of the impurities. After that, the molten silver, or *batch,* was poured into another pan and allowed to cool.

After the batch had cooled and hardened, it was rubbed on a flintlike stone called a *touchstone.* The streak that the batch made on the stone was then compared to that of pure silver. If the two marks did not agree, the batch was remelted and the process was repeated until the streaks looked alike. Once the silver was refined

*A silversmith
casting melted silver in
a mold, or ingot.*

to an absolutely pure state, it was much too soft
to be of any practical use. Remelting it and add-
ing a small amount of copper hardened it, however, and made it more durable.

The *TECHNIQUE*

A careful measuring of the mixture, or *alloy,*
of silver and copper was most important, since
the quality of silver was determined by the
amount of added copper. The best colonial American silver contained, out of every 1,000 parts,
925 parts of pure silver and 75 parts of pure
copper. This proportion made a silver equal to
English sterling, known as the finest silver in the
world. The perfect melting together, or fusion, of
925 parts of silver and 75 parts of copper was
called the *true standard.*

Once the silver was refined and brought to the
true standard, it was heated and poured into an
ingot, or mold, then was allowed to cool and
harden. This process was called *casting.* The ingot
made a blocklike bar of silver. Once hardened,
the bar was removed from the mold, but was
still called an ingot. Thus an ingot of silver usually meant a bar of silver. It was a shape handy
to store away for future use, but had nothing

*Making ready
to pound an ingot of silver
into a plate.*

The TECHNIQUE

whatever to do with the shape of the silver piece that might finally be made from it.

When the silversmith was ready to make a silver object, he placed the ingot on a large iron block called an *anvil*. Because silver is a soft metal, it can be pounded into sheets. It is quite possible, for example, to pound pure silver into sheets so thin that one million of them piled one on top of another would not measure 12 inches high. Silver so pounded is called *silver leaf*.

Silver leaf by itself is fragile and cannot be shaped into a durable object. But the silversmith who was making a bowl or cup was not pounding pure silver on his iron anvil. He was working with an ingot of silver-copper alloy, somewhat harder than pure silver. By constantly reheating the ingot without melting it, and by pounding it while it was red hot, he was able to make a sheet of the thickness he needed.

Heating and pounding a bar of silver into a sheet was called *forging*. The work was done on a *forging anvil*. The silver sheet itself was called a *plate*.

Using a special pair of scissors, or *shears,* the

The TECHNIQUE

silversmith next cut a circular shape out of the plate. He had previously prepared a drawing of the piece he was about to make. A *cross-section plan* showed its exact size in outline. Before cutting the metal, he had carefully measured the entire outline of the piece he was planning. The sum of all the parts measured was equal to the *diameter* of the circular plate, or the width through its center.

With his compasses the silversmith then *engraved,* or cut, into the plate a set of circles, one within another, all with the same central point. This central point was also the exact center of the circular plate. The engraved circles were hardly noticeable, but they served the silversmith as guidelines in shaping his piece.

The round plate was then placed on a small iron block called a *raising anvil,* where it was *raised,* or delicately hammered, into the desired form. In order to keep the plate soft enough to work, and to prevent it from becoming too brittle from the constant hammerblows, continual reheating was needed. This reheating, or *annealing,* as it was called, also toughened, or *tempered,*

The *TECHNIQUE*

the metal. The annealing ended when the plate reached the exact size and shape the silversmith wanted.

Further shaping of the piece was done with various tools and anvils. The silversmith used *stakes,* or small upright anvils, and *beakhorns,* sharply pointed anvils that enabled him to work the inside of a cup or bowl.

The hammer marks were removed from the piece and it was brought to a mirrorlike finish by delicately tapping its surface with special hammers, on special anvils called *planishing anvils* and in special shallow vessels called *planishing tests.* These hammers, anvils, and tests all had highly polished surfaces. Great skill and patience were needed in using them.

Small parts, such as spouts, handles, hinges, and covers, were separately cast in molds held in iron frames, called *casting flasks.* These parts were fused or soldered onto the main form.

Stringlike moldings for rims and decorations were made with a machine called a *drawing bench.* Here a strip of silver was drawn or pulled through an exactly measured opening formed by

The *TECHNIQUE*

drawing irons. When the desired length was reached, the drawn molding was soldered onto the piece.

Decoration was sometimes hammered into the piece from the inside. This was called *embossing.* Designs were also engraved or punched into the surface of the piece with sharp knives called *gravers,* or with blunt metal rods called *chasing punches.* This kind of decoration was known as *chasing.*

When the silversmith wanted to chase a piece, he first packed the inside of a hollow object — or the back side of a flat object — with pitch, a tarlike substance. This packing prevented unnecessary denting. After the decoration was completed, the silversmith removed the packing and gave the piece a final polishing with smooth stones called *burnishing stones* and with *pumice,* a fine volcanic powder.

He then struck his mark on the piece, so identifying himself as its maker, and guaranteeing its high quality. Then, and only then, was his work finished and the customer notified that the piece was ready. He, as owner, returned to the

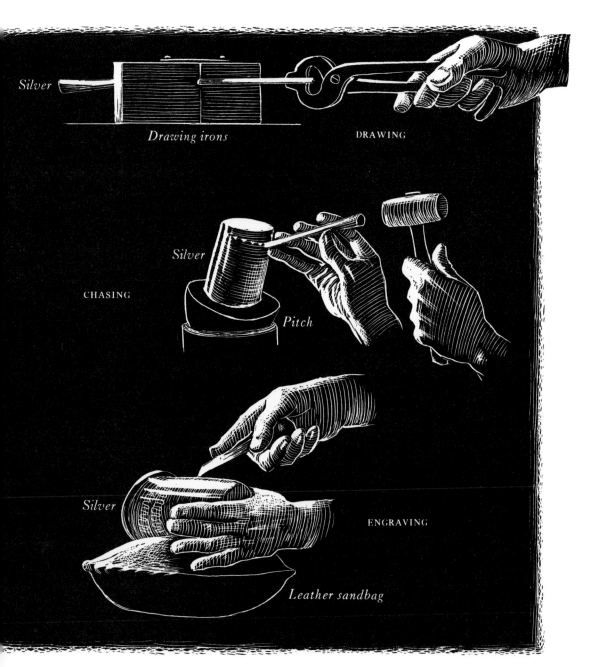

Silver

Drawing irons   DRAWING

Silver

CHASING

Pitch

Silver

ENGRAVING

Leather sandbag

shop and paid the silversmith for his labors. The piece now belonged to him and to all those who would come after him.

The *TECHNIQUE*

The colonial American silversmith was proud of his knowledge and ability. He created silver pieces with such patient care that many of them are used and admired to this day.

And just as he advertised, his pieces were "as good as sterling." He was true to his word and craft. Colonial American silver was indeed the equal of the world's finest silver.

Silversmiths' Terms

ALLOY — A mixture of metals.

ANNEALING — The softening of metal by reheating.

ANVIL — An iron block used to hammer out metal and shape it.

BATCH — A quantity of molten silver.

BEAKHORN — A sharply pointed iron block (a kind of anvil).

BURNISHING — Polishing.

CASTING — Pouring of hot liquid metal into a mold and letting it harden into the wanted shape.

CASTING FLASKS — Iron frames to hold molds for small parts.

CHASING — Ornamental engraving or punching.

DRAWING BENCH — A machine for pulling silver into strings or strips.

DRAWING IRONS — Metal parts on a drawing bench, through which silver is drawn.

EMBOSSING — Hammering a decoration on an object from the inside out.

ENGRAVING — Cutting lines into a metal surface.

FORGING — The shaping of metal by heating and hammering.

INGOT — A bar of silver (also, sometimes, the bar mold).

PLANISHING — Making smooth.

PLANISHING TEST — A shallow cup or vessel used to smooth metal.

PLATE — A sheet of silver.

RAISING — The hammering of a plate into an object.

STAKES — Small iron posts of varying sizes, used as anvils.

STERLING — The standard of fineness of English silver: 925 parts silver, 75 parts copper.

TEMPERING — The toughening of metal by heat.

TOUCHSTONE — A flintlike stone used to determine the purity of gold or silver.

TRUE STANDARD — The fusion of 925 parts of silver and 75 parts of copper.

Some Colonial American Silversmiths and Their Marks*

JOSIAH AUSTIN
  Charlestown, Massachusetts

HENRICUS BOELEN
  New York, N.Y.

JOHN BURT
  Boston, Massachusetts

JOHN CODDINGTON
  Newport, Rhode Island

JOHN CONEY
  Boston, Massachusetts

JOHN DE NISE
  Philadelphia, Pennsylvania

JEREMIAH DUMMER
  Boston, Massachusetts

JOHN EDWARDS
  Boston, Massachusetts

RENE GRIGNON
  Norwich, Connecticut

JOHN HULL
  Boston, Massachusetts

* *Full names or last names only were struck after 1725.*

JACOB HURD
  Boston, Massachusetts

JOHN INCH
  Annapolis, Maryland

CORNELIUS KIERSTEDE
  New York, N.Y., and later,
  New Haven, Connecticut

MYER MYERS
  New York, N.Y.

JOHANNIS NYS
  Philadelphia, Pennsylvania

JOHN POTWINE
  Hartford, Connecticut

JOB PRINCE
  Milford, Connecticut

PETER QUINTARD
  New York, N.Y., and later,
  South Norwalk, Connecticut

PAUL REVERE
  Boston, Massachusetts

FRANCIS RICHARDSON
  Philadelphia, Pennsylvania

NICHOLAS ROOSEVELT
New York, N.Y.

ROBERT SANDERSON
  Boston, Massachusetts

ENOCH STANTON
Stonington, Connecticut

LUKE STOUTENBURGH
Charleston, South Carolina

BARENT TEN EYCK
Albany, New York

CORNELIUS VANDERBURGH
New York, N.Y.

JACOBUS VAN DER SPIEGEL
New York, N.Y.

NICHOLAS VAN RENSSALAER
Albany, N.Y.

BILIOUS WARD
Guilford, Connecticut

EDWARD WINSLOW
Boston, Massachusetts

BANCROFT WOODCOCK
Wilmington, Delaware

ANTIPAS WOODWARD
Middletown, Connecticut

BENJAMIN WYNKOOP
New York, N.Y.

EBENEZER YOUNG
Hebron, Connecticut

Index

LEONARD EVERETT FISHER is a well-known author-artist whose books include *Alphabet Art, The Great Wall of China, The Tower of London, Marie Curie, Jason and the Golden Fleece, The Olympians, The ABC Exhibit, Sailboat Lost,* and many others.

Often honored for his contribution to children's literature, Mr. Fisher was the recipient of the 1989 Nonfiction Award presented by the *Washington Post* and the Children's Book Guild of Washington for the body of an author's work. In 1991, he received both the Catholic Library Association's Regina Medal and the University of Minnesota's Kerlan Award for the entire body of his work. Leonard Everett Fisher lives in Westport, Connecticut.

The text of this book has been composed on the linotype in Caslon 137. This face is derived from the great oldstyle cut by William Caslon of London in the early eighteenth century. Caslon types were used widely by American printers during the colonial period and even today it is considered to be "the finest vehicle for the conveyance of English speech that the art of the punch-cutter has yet devised."